Highlights of English Literature

Edited by **Sue Hackman**

Hodder Education

A MEMBER OF HACHETTE LIVRE UK

Photo credits and acknowledgements can be found on p. 89

Orders: please contact Bookpoint Ltd, 130 Milton Park, Abingdon, Oxon
OX14 4SB. Telephone: (44) 01235 827720. Fax: (44) 01235 400454. Lines are
open 9.00–5.00, Monday to Saturday, with a 24-hour message answering
service. Visit our website at www.hoddereducation.co.uk

Impression number   5 4 3 2 1
Year   2012 2011 2010 2009 2008

Cover photo: Lynn James/Photonica/Getty Images
Typeset in 12/14pt Bembo by Charon Tec Ltd (A Macmillan Company),
Chennai, India
www.charontec.com

Printed in Great Britain by CPI Antony Rowe.

A catalogue record for this title is available from the British Library

ISBN: 978 0340 966 327

Contents

The 1900s   **65**

Introduction

Literature offers a glimpse into the past – not only in what it tells us, but in the way it tells us. We take a privileged glimpse into the minds of people who lived before us, so we can experience again the way they felt, saw and understood things, and to feel their words rolling around our own mouths.

I chose the extracts in groups, to reflect the style and preoccupations of the centuries in which they were written and to be accessible to those who are encountering older language for the first time. I tried to keep to well-known writers, and I excluded writers born on other continents, though I may have cheated once or twice.

I apologise to all the great and worthy writers I left out.

Sue Hackman
January 2008

Before 1500

So few people were literate before 1500 that literature was written to be performed and heard, rather than read. Noblemen and monks learned to read, but most ordinary people were peasants who worked the land and never attended school. They did not learn to read or write, and they worked hard and died young. We know that stories, songs and poems were learned by heart and circulated by word of mouth. Bible stories were well-known from church, and travelling entertainers were popular, performing plays and singing for crowds, or to rich people in their houses. So people in the Middle Ages did have literature; they just didn't write it down.

Much of the written literature that has survived is poetry, and most of it was set to music. In poetry, you are reading song lyrics! It takes some effort to read them because the words and sentences of the English language have changed over time. Most of this poetry is anonymous (*Anon*); we don't know who composed it or who wrote it down. We don't even know the year in which these poems were written, but they have been arranged in rough chronological order.

Chaucer is the first giant name in English literature because, even after 600 years, we can (with a little effort) follow his words straight off the page.

Fowls in the frith

This poem seems to describe the thoughts of someone who is contemplating nature and his own state of mind.

Fowls in the **frith**,
Fishes in the flood,
And I must **wax wod**:
Much sorrow I walk with
For best of bone and blood.

Anon

frith – wood
wax wod – go mad

The Squire

In The Canterbury Tales, *Chaucer wrote about a group of pilgrims travelling to a shrine in Canterbury, all telling each other stories along the way. In the* General Prologue, *he describes the pilgrims one by one. Here is a description of the Squire.*

With hym ther was his sone, a yong squier,
A lovyere and a lusty bacheler,
With **lokkes crulle** as they were **leyd in presse**.
Of twenty yeer of age he was, I gesse.
Of his stature he was of **evene lengthe**,
And wonderly **delyvere**, and of greet strengthe.
And he hadde been somtyme in **chyvachie**
In Flaundres, in Artoys, and Pycardie,
And **born hym weel**, as of so **litel space**,
In hope to stonden in his lady grace.

2

Embrouded was he, as it were a **meede**
Al ful of fresshe floures, whyte and reede.
Syngynge he was, or **floytynge**, al the day;
He was as fressh as is the month of May.
Short was his gowne, with sleves longe and wyde.
Wel koude he sitte on hors and faire ryde.
He koude songes make and wel **endite**,
Juste and **eek** daunce, and weel **purtreye** and write.
So **hoote** he lovede that by **nyghtertale**
He sleep namoore than dooth a nyghtyngale.
Curteis he was, lowely, and servysable,
And **carf biforn** his fader at the table.

From The Canterbury Tales *by Geoffrey Chaucer*

lokkes crulle – curly hair
leyd in presse – curled
evene lengthe – medium height
delyvere – fit
chyvachie – the cavalry
born hym weel – did well
litel space – short time
embrouded – embroidered
meede – meadow
floytynge – playing the flute or whistling
endite – compose lyrics
juste – joust
eek – also
purtreye – paint and draw
hoote – hotly, passionately
nyghtertale – night-time
curteis – courteous, polite
carf biforn – carved the meat

Summer is icumen in

This poem, which celebrates the start of summer, was often sung in a round.

Summer is **icumen** in,
Loud sing cuckoo!
Groweth seed and bloweth mead
And springeth wood anew.
Sing cuckoo!

Ewe bleateth after lamb,
Cow loweth after calf,
Bullock starteth, buck verteth,
Merry sing cuckoo!

Cuckoo, cuckoo!
Well singest thou cuckoo,
Not cease thou never now!

Sing cuckoo now, sing cuckoo!
Sing cuckoo, sing cuckoo now!

Summer is icumen manuscript from the British Library.

Anon

icumen – coming, arriving

Lord thou clepedest me

This is a religious poem.

Lord, thou **clepedest** me,
And I naught ne answered Thee
But wordes slow and sleepy:
'**Thole** yet! Thole a little!'
But 'yet' and 'yet' was endless,
And 'thole a little' a long way is.

Anon

clepedest – called
thole – wait

Peace maketh plenty

Peace maketh plenty;
Plenty maketh pride;
Pride maketh plea;
Plea maketh povert;
Povert maketh peace.

Anon

I have been a foster

This is a forester's song about his dream to retire and live in a house in the woods.

I have been a **foster** long and many day;
My lockes be **hoar**
I shall hang up my horn by the greenwood spray;
Foster will I be no more.
All the while that I may my bow bend
Shall I wedde no wife
I shall **bigge** me a **bower** at the woode's end
There to lead my life.

Anon

foster – forester
hoar – white
bigge – build
bower – a summer house

My love ys faren in a lond

A man misses his lover when she is away

My love is **faren** in a land:
Alas why is she so?
And I am so **sore bound**
I may not come her to.
She hath my heart in hold
Wherever she ride or go,
With true love a thousandfold.

Anon

faren – travelling
sore bound – stuck here

Western Wind

This is a poem for a wet day when you just want to go back to bed.

Western wind when wilt thou blow?
The small rain down can rain!
Christ if my love were in my arms
And I in my bed again.

Anon

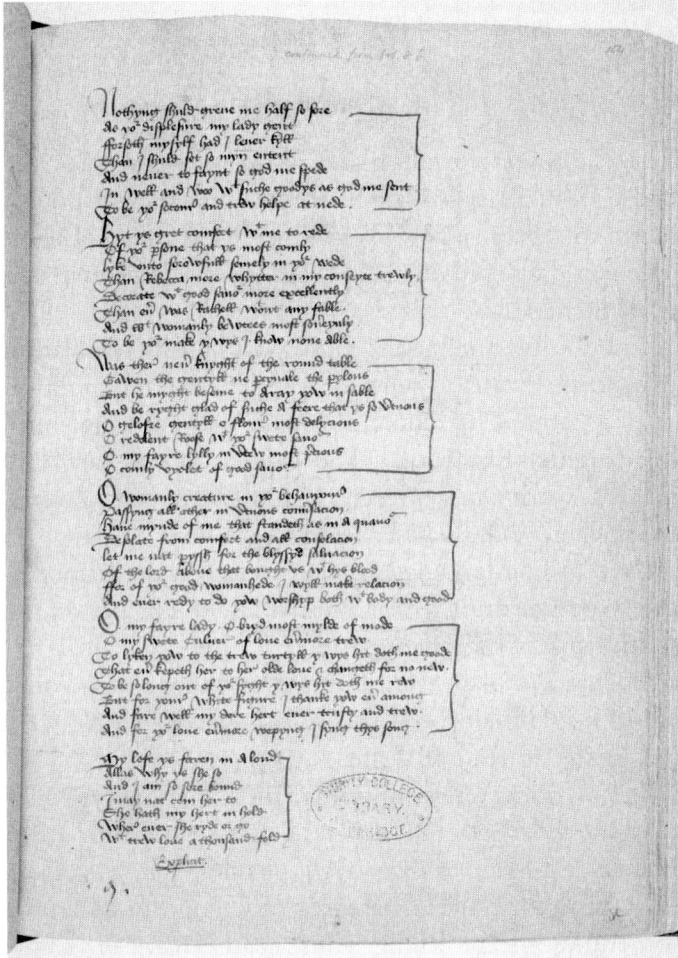

My love ys faren in a lond manuscript from Trinity College, Cambridge.

The 1500s

The 1500s were exciting and prosperous times. Society had been unchanged for hundreds of years, but now it began to develop a new class of merchants and craftsmen. The world opened out as new lands were discovered and trade increased.

London became a very busy port and its population expanded. It was a centre of commerce and political activity around the court of Henry VIII and, after him, his daughter Elizabeth I. The citizens of this new city needed work and entertainment. There were taverns everywhere and the first theatres were built. Shakespeare arrived in London and his plays were first performed at the Rose Theatre, then later at the Globe Theatre on the south bank of the Thames.

Poetry and plays were popular, and those who could afford it sent their sons to schools, but most people were still unable to read or write.

It was, nonetheless, an uneasy time. There were social tensions between the different faiths, and war with France and Spain was always a possibility. It was also a risky time for political advisers, as falling out of favour sometimes meant losing your head. However, clever people could make a good living in public service, or working for rich men.

Sighs are my food

Sir Thomas Wyatt was an ambassador – some would say a spy – and was once accused of treason and on another occasion of being Ann Boleyn's lover. He wrote this poem to his son Brian while he was locked up in prison.

Sighs are my food, drink are my tears,
Clinking of **fetters** such music would crave;
Stink and close air away my life wears,
Innocency is all the hope I have;
Rain, wind, or weather I judge by mine ears;
Malice assaulted that righteousness should have.
Sure I am, Brian, this wound shall heal again,
But yet, alas, the scar shall still remain.

Sir Thomas Wyatt, around 1540

fetters – chains

Portrait of Sir Thomas Wyatt.

Thousandes have famishede

This poem is a complaint to the rich and powerful about their treatment of the poor.

Thousandes have famishede for food,
    And thousandes mor be **lek**,
Change nowe therfor your crewell moode,
    And them to sucoure sek.

Thousandes ar **pyned** to the bonys
    With hongge, thrist and cold;
And thousands in strong fettars gronnes
    Yowe caus thereof behold.

The fatharles and wydowe pore,
    The syk, the sor, the lame,
Ly dyeng nowe at every dore,
    And **non by youe** in blame.

Anon, around 1550

lek – *probably meaning* in the same position
pyned – lost the will to live
non by youe – you feel no blame

My true-love hath my heart

This is a love sonnet, often recited at weddings.

My true-love hath my heart, and I have his,
By just exchange one for the other given.
I hold his dear, and mine he cannot miss:
There never was a bargain better driven.
His heart in me keeps me and him in one;
My heart in him his thoughts and senses guides:
He loves my heart, for once it was his own;

I cherish his because in me it bides.
His heart his wound received from my sight;
My heart was wounded with his wounded heart;
For as from me on him his hurt did light,
So still, methought, in me his hurt did smart:
Both equal hurt, in this change sought our bliss,
My true love hath my heart and I have his.

Sir Philip Sidney, around 1577

Drunkeness

This is a factual account of English drinking habits in the sixteenth century.

Every country, city, town, village and other places hath abundance of alehouses, taverns and inns, which are so fraught with malt-worms, night and day, that you would wonder to see them. You shall have them there sitting at the wine and good-ale all day long, yea, all the night too, peradventure a whole week together, so long as any money is left; swilling, gulling and carousing from one to another, till never a one can speak a ready word. Then, when with the spirit of the buttery they are thus possessed, a world it is to consider their gestures and demeanours, one towards another and towards everyone else. How they stut and stammer, stagger and reel to and fro like madmen, and which is most horrible, some fall to swearing, cursing and banning, interlacing their speeches with curious terms of blasphemy, to the great dishonour of God, and offence of the godly ears present.

Philip Stubbes, 1583

Epigram

This poem was written by an earl who was a courtier in the Royal Court during Queen Elizabeth I's reign.

Were I a king, I might command content,
Were I obscure, unknown would be my cares,
And were I dead, no thoughts should me torment,
Nor words, nor wrongs, nor loves, nor hate, nor fears.
A doubtful choice for me, of three things one to crave:
A kingdom, or a cottage, or a grave.

Edward de Vere, Earl of Oxford, around 1590

Henry V makes a speech to his army

Shakespeare's play is based on the life of Henry V, and a real event: the Battle of Agincourt, which Henry won despite being outnumbered one to five by the French enemy. The battle was fought on 25 October 1415. It was St Crispin's Day. In this scene, Henry lifts the spirit of his troops by offering them escape at the same time as hope of a famous victory.

WESTMORELAND:
O that we now had here
But one ten thousand of those men in England
That do no work to-day!

KING HENRY V:
What's he that wishes so?
My cousin Westmoreland? No, my fair cousin:
If we are mark'd to die, we are **enow**
To do our country loss; and if to live,

The fewer men, the greater share of honour.
God's will! I pray thee, wish not one man more.
By Jove, I am not **covetous** for gold,
Nor care I who doth feed upon my cost;
It yearns me not if men my garments wear;
Such outward things dwell not in my desires:
But if it be a sin to covet honour,
I am the most offending soul alive.
No, faith, **my coz**, wish not a man from England:
God's peace! I would not lose so great an honour
As one man more, methinks, would share from me
For the best hope I have. O, do not wish one more!
Rather proclaim it, Westmoreland, through my host,
That he which hath no stomach to this fight,
Let him depart; his passport shall be made
And **crowns for convoy** put into his purse:
We would not die in that man's company
That fears his fellowship to die with us.
This day is called the feast of Crispian:
He that outlives this day, and comes safe home,
Will stand a tip-toe when the day is named,
And rouse him at the name of Crispian.
He that shall live this day, and see old age,
Will yearly on the vigil feast his neighbours,
And say 'To-morrow is Saint Crispian':
Then will he strip his sleeve and show his scars.
And say 'These wounds I had on Crispin's day.'
Old men forget: yet all shall be forgot,
But he'll remember with advantages
What feats he did that day: then shall our names.
Familiar in his mouth as household words
Harry the king, Bedford and Exeter,
Warwick and Talbot, Salisbury and Gloucester,

Be in their flowing cups freshly remember'd.
This story shall the good man teach his son;
And Crispin Crispian shall ne'er go by,
From this day to the ending of the world,
But we in it shall be remember'd;
We few, we happy few, we band of brothers;
For he to-day that sheds his blood with me
Shall be my brother; be he ne'er so vile,
This day shall **gentle his condition**:
And gentlemen in England now a-bed
Shall think themselves accursed they were not here,
And hold their manhoods cheap whiles any speaks
That fought with us upon Saint Crispin's day.

From Henry V
by William Shakespeare, 1599

enow – enough **crowns for convoy** – money to escape
covetous – greedy **gentle his condition** – be made a nobleman
my coz – cousin

Battle scene from the 1989 film adaptation of *Henry V*.

The 1600s

The 1600s, known as the Stuart period, were a time of political and social upheaval. There was a civil war, which led to the execution of King Charles I, and for a few years England was a republic.

It was an insecure and unsettling time. There were spies everywhere and wars abroad. People feared that England would be invaded. Plagues swept across Europe. There were witch hunts. The great fire of London burned down a large part of the city.

Writers did not always know how far they could go before they offended someone. A great deal of literature in this period is inspired by religion, but there is also a strong feeling of insecurity and a sense that life is fragile. Writers were not simply afraid of death, but of what might lie on the other side.

Most of the great writers of the day were working in London, which was huge by the standards of the time. It was a golden age of theatre: Shakespeare was writing his tragedies, and other playwrights (such as Christopher Marlowe) were popular too. Poets discovered that they could use their writing to promote their views and beliefs.

Faustus's final hour

In this play, Faustus sells his soul to the Devil in return for a life of luxury in which all his wishes come true. But now his time is up, and he waits for devils to collect him and carry him off to Hell. Faustus is speaking his thoughts aloud.

O Faustus,
Now hast thou but one bare hour to live,
And then thou must be damn'd perpetually!
Stand still, you ever-moving **spheres of heaven**,
That time may cease, and midnight never come;
Fair Nature's eye, rise, rise again, and make
Perpetual day; or let this hour be but
A year, a month, a week, a natural day,
That Faustus may repent and save his soul!
O lente, lente currite, noctis equi!
The stars move still, time runs, the clock will strike,
The devil will come, and Faustus must be damn'd.
O, I'll leap up to heaven! – Who pulls me down? –
See, where Christ's blood streams in the firmament!
One drop of blood will save me: O my Christ! –
Rend not my heart for naming of my Christ;
Yet will I call on him: O, spare me, Lucifer! –
Where is it now? 'tis gone:
And, see, a threatening arm, an angry brow!
Mountains and hills, come, come, and fall on me,
And hide me from the heavy wrath of heaven!
No!
Then will I headlong run into the earth:
Earth, gape! O, no, it will not harbour me!
You stars that reign'd at my nativity,

Whose influence hath allotted death and hell,
Now draw up Faustus, like a foggy mist,
Into the entrails of yon labouring clouds,
That, when you vomit forth into the air,
My limbs may issue from your smoky mouths;
But let my soul mount and ascend to heaven!

The clock strikes the half-hour.

O, half the hour is past! 'twill all be past anon.
O, if my soul must suffer for my sin,
Impose some end to my incessant pain;
Let Faustus live in hell a thousand years,
A hundred thousand, and at last be sav'd!
No end is limited to damned souls.
Why wert thou not a creature **wanting soul**?
Or why is this immortal that thou hast?
O, **Pythagoras' metempsychosis**, were that true,
This soul should fly from me, and I be chang'd
Into some brutish beast! all beasts are happy,
For, when they die,
Their souls are soon dissolv'd in elements;
But mine must live still to be plagu'd in hell.
Curs'd be the parents that engender'd me!
No, Faustus, curse thyself, curse **Lucifer**
That hath depriv'd thee of the joys of heaven.

The clock strikes twelve.

It strikes, it strikes! Now, body, turn to air,
Or Lucifer will bear thee quick to hell!
O soul, be chang'd into small water-drops,
And fall into the ocean, ne'er be found!

17

Thunder. Enter DEVILS.

O, mercy, heaven! look not so fierce on me!
Adders and serpents, let me breathe awhile!
Ugly hell, gape not! come not, Lucifer!
I'll burn my books! – O **Mephistophilis**!

Exeunt DEVILS with FAUSTUS.

From **The Tragical History of Doctor Faustus**
by Christopher Marlowe, 1604

spheres of heaven – movement of moon and stars
O lente, lente currite, noctis equi! – Run slowly, slowly, horses of the
night!
rend not – do not tear apart
wanting soul – without a soul
Pythagoras metempsychosis – the theory that after death you are reborn
as a lower lifeform
Lucifer – the Devil
Mephistophilis – one of the Devil's main helpers

London streets

This is a factual account of busy London life.

In every street, carts and coaches make such a thundering
as if the world ran upon wheels: at every corner, men,
women and children meet in such shoals, that posts are
set up of purpose to strengthen the houses, lest with
jostling one another they should shoulder them down.
Besides, hammers are beating in one place, **tubs hooping** in another, pots clinking in a third, water-tankards
running at tilt in a fourth. Here are porters sweating
under burdens, their merchant's man bearing bags of

Engraving of London Bridge and the City in Stuart times.

money. **Chapmen** (as if they were at leap frog) skip out of one shop into another. Tradesmen (as if they were dancing **galliards**) are **lusty at legs** and never stand still. All are as busy as country **attorneys at assizes**.

From The Seven Deadly Sinnes of London
by Thomas Dekker, 1606

tubs hooping – making barrels by fixing metal hoops around them
chapmen – book salesmen
galliard – a kind of dance
lusty at legs – always on the go
attorneys at assizes – lawyers in court

No man is an island

John Donne is famous for the love poems of his youth, and later for his religious poetry. He was the Dean of St Paul's Cathedral in London. This is one of his 'Meditations', a

19

cross between a sermon and a prayer. The bell is the church bell rung on important occasions such as funerals.

He for whom this bell tolls may be so ill as that he knows not it tolls for him; and **perchance** I may think myself so much better than I am, as that they who are about me and see my state may have caused it to toll for me, and I know not that. The church is universal, so are all her actions; all that she does belongs to all. When she baptizes a child, that action concerns me; for that child is thereby connected to that **head** which is my head too. And when she buries a man, that action concerns me: all mankind is of one author and is one volume; when one man dies, one chapter is not torn out of the book, but translated into a better language; and every chapter must be so translated. Therefore the bell that rings a sermon calls not upon the preacher only, but upon the congregation to come, so this bell calls us all; but how much more me, who am brought so near the door by this sickness. The bell doth toll for him that thinks it doth. Who casts not up his eye to the sun when it rises? but who takes off his eye from a comet when that breaks out? Who bends not his ear to any bell which upon any occasion rings? but who can remove it from that bell which is passing a piece of himself out of this world? No man is an island, entire of itself; every man is a piece of the continent, a part of the **main**. If a clod be washed away by the sea, Europe is the less. Any man's death diminishes me, because I am involved in mankind; and therefore never send to know for whom the bell tolls; it tolls for thee.

Abridged from 'Meditation XVII'
by John Donne, 1624

perchance – maybe
head – leadership of the church
main – mainland

Sic Vita (Such is life)

Francis Beaumont compares the shortness of man's life with other brief, beautiful events in nature.

Like to the falling of a Starre;
Or as the flights of eagles are;
Or like the fresh sprigs **gawdy hew**;
Or silver drops of morning dew;
Or like a wind that **chafes** the flood;
Or bubbles which on water stood;
Even such is man, whose borrow'd light
Is straight call'd in, and paid to night.

The wind blowes out; the Bubble dies;
The Spring entomb'd in Autumn lie;
The Dew dries up; the Starre is shot;
The Flight is past; and Man forgot.

Francis Beaumont, 1640

gawdy hew – bright colours
chafes – ripples the surface

Upon Julia's clothes

In this poem, the poet imagines the woman of his dreams taking off her clothes.

Whenas in silks my Julia goes,
Then, then, methinks, how sweetly flows
That liquefaction of her clothes.

21

Next, when I cast mine eyes and see
That brave vibration each way free;
O how that glittering taketh me!

Robert Herrick, around 1648

Mediocrity in love rejected

This is a sonnet.

Give me more Love, or more Disdain;
The Torrid, or the Frozen Zone
Bring equall ease unto my paine;
The Temperate affords me none:
Either extreme, of Love, or Hate,
Is sweeter than a calme estate.

Give me a storme; if it be Love,
Like *Danae* in that golden showre
I swim in pleasure; if it prove
Disdain, that Torrent will devour
My Vulture-hopes; and he's possest
Of Heaven, that's but from Hell releast:
Then crown my joyes, or cure my pain;
Give me more Love, or more Disdain.

Thomas Carew, 1640

Danae in that golden showre – legend has it that Danae was blessed with
a gift of money by the gods, who sent a shower of coins to rain on her.

Samuel Pepys digs up his gold

This is the 10 October 1667 entry of Samuel Pepys, who kept a secret diary written in code. It is the first really personal diary published in English. Some months before, his father and his wife buried the family gold in the garden while Pepys was absent, because they thought that England was about to be invaded by the Dutch. The danger having passed, Pepys decides to dig it up. W. Hewer was Pepys' assistant.

10th October 1667

Up, to walk up and down the garden with my father, to talk of all our concernments: about a husband for my sister, whereof there is at present no appearance, but we must endeavour to find her one now, for she grows old and ugly. My father and I with a dark lantern, it now being night, into the garden with my wife, and there went about our great work to dig up my gold. But Lord! What a **toss** I was for some time in, that they could not justly tell where it was, that I begun heartily to sweat and be angry, that they should not agree better upon the place, and at last to fear that it was gone: but by and by poking with a **spit**, we found it, and then begun with a **spud** to lift up the ground. But, good God! to see how sillily they did it, not a half a foot underground, and in the sight of the world from a hundred places, if anybody by accident were near hand, and within sight of a neighbour's window; only my father says that he saw them all gone to church before he began the work, when he laid the money. But I was out of my wits almost, and the more from that, upon my lifting up the earth with the spud, I did discern that I scattered the

23

pieces of gold round about the ground among the grass and loose earth. And taking up the iron head-pieces wherein they were put, I perceived the earth was got among the gold, and wet, so that the bags were all rotten, and all the notes, that I could not tell what in the world to say to it, not knowing how to judge what was wanting or what had been lost which, all put together, did make me mad; and at last I was forced to take up the head-pieces, dirt and all, and as many of the scattered pieces as I could with the dirt discern by candlelight, and carry them up into my brother's chamber, and there did lock them up till I had eat a little supper.

And then, all people going to bed, W. Hewer and I did all alone, with several pails of water and **besoms**, at last wash the dirt off the pieces, and parted the pieces and the dirt, and then began to tell them, by a note which I had of the value of the whole, in my pocket; and do find that there was short above a hundred pieces, which did make me mad; and considering that the neighbour's house was so near, that we could not suppose we could speak to one another in the garden at that place where the gold lay – especially my father being deaf – but they must know what we had been doing, I feared that they might in the night come and gather some pieces and prevent us the next morning; so W. Hewer and I went out again about midnight, for it was now grown so late, and there by candle-light did make shift to gather forty-five pieces more. And so in, and to cleanse them; and by this time it was past two in the morning; and so to bed, with my mind pretty quiet that I have recovered so many. And lay there in some disquiet all night, telling of the clock till it was daylight.

From **The Diary** *by Samuel Pepys, 1667*

toss – panic
spit – iron stick
spud – spade
besoms – brooms

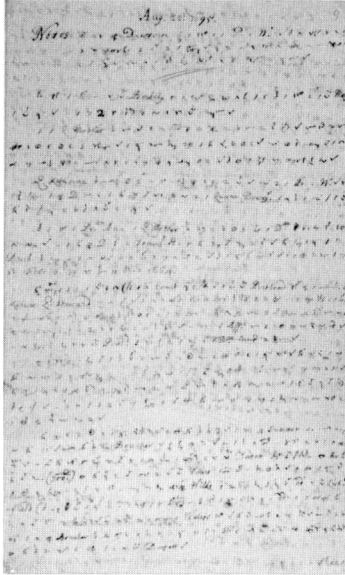

A sample of Pepys' writing in code.

Better to reign in Hell, than serve in Heaven

In this extract from John Milton's long poem, Paradise
Lost, *Lucifer the rebel angel has been thrown out of heaven
by God. He is looking around at Hell, where he will
become better known as the Devil, talking up the benefits
of spending eternity there.*

'Is this the region, this the soil, the **clime**,'
Said then the lost **archangel**, 'this the seat
That we must change for heav'n, this mournful
  gloom

25

Engraving by Gustave Doré of Lucifer's fall from Heaven.

For that **celestial** light? Be it so, since he
Who now is **sovran** can dispose and bid
What shall be right: **fardest** from him is best
Whom reason hath equalled, force hath made
  supreme
Above his equals. Farewell happy fields
Where joy for ever dwells: Hail, horrors, hail,
Infernal world, and thou, profoundest hell
Receive thy new possessor: One who brings
A mind not to be chang'd by place or time.
The mind is its own place, and in itself
Can make a heav'n of hell, a hell of heav'n.
What matter where, if I be still the same,
And what I should be, all but less than he
Whom thunder hath made greater? Here at least

We shall be free; th' Almighty hath not built
Here for his envy, will not drive us hence:
Here we may reign secure, and in my choice
To reign is worth ambition though in hell:
Better to reign in hell, than serve in heav'n.'

From **Paradise Lost** *by John Milton, 1667*

clime – climate
archangel – high-ranking angel
celestial – heavenly
sovran – ruler
fardest – furthest

Upon a snail

She goes but softly, but she goeth sure;
    She stumbles not as stronger creatures do:
Her journey's shorter, so she may endure
    Better than they which do much further go.

She makes no noise, but **stilly seizeth** on
    The flower or herb appointed for her food,
The which she quietly doth feed upon,
    While others **range and gare**, but find no good.

And though she doth but very softly go,
    However 'tis not fast, nor slow, but sure;
And certainly they that do travel so,
    The prize they do aim at they do procure.

John Bunyan, 1686

stilly seizeth – can grip
range and gare – graze

The 1700s

The 1700s were a more stable period in English history. Trade thrived and ships travelled the world to find new goods and markets. England began to build its empire. It was the start of the slave trade.

Machines were invented to save work, canals were dug out and the first factories were built – industry grew. Merchants, tradesmen, shopkeepers and a small class of professional people prospered, and education spread as the 'middle' class began to grow.

The theatre continued to attract big audiences, and witty comedies were popular. There were also many writers of prose, partly because there were more people to read their work. Up to this period, prose had been almost entirely non-fiction, often about politics or religion, but now the first works of fiction began to emerge.

Robinson Crusoe is almost drowned

The novel Robinson Crusoe *is often said to be the first proper novel in English. Based on a true story, it tells the story of a man lost on a desert island for twenty two years. This extract describes him fighting for his life after being shipwrecked.*

Nothing can describe the Confusion of Thought which I felt when I sunk into the Water; for tho' I swam very well, yet I could not deliver my self from the Waves so as to draw Breath, till that Wave having driven me, or rather carried me a vast Way on towards the Shore, and having spent itself, went back, and left me upon the Land almost dry, but half-dead with the Water I took in. I had so much Presence of Mind as well as Breath left, that seeing my self nearer the main Land than I expected, I got upon my Feet, and endeavoured to make on towards the Land as fast as I could, before another Wave should return, and take me up again. But I soon found it was impossible to avoid it; for I saw the Sea come after me as high as a great Hill, and as furious as an Enemy which I had no Means or Strength to contend with; my Business was to hold my Breath, and raise my self upon the Water, if I could; and so by swimming to preserve my Breathing, and Pilot my self towards the Shore, if possible; my greatest Concern now being, that the Sea, as it would carry me a great Way towards the Shore when it came on, might not carry me back again with it when it gave back towards the Sea.

The Wave that came upon me again, buried me at once 20 or 30 Foot deep in its own Body; and I could feel my self carried with a mighty Force and Swiftness towards the Shore a very great Way; but I held my Breath, and assisted my self to swim still forward with all my Might. I was ready to burst with holding my Breath, when, as I felt my self rising up, so to my immediate Relief, I found my Head and Hands shoot out above the Surface of the Water; and tho' it was not two Seconds of Time that I could keep my self so, yet it reliev'd me greatly, gave me Breath and new Courage. I was covered again with Water a good while, but not so long but I held it out; and finding the Water had spent it self, and began to return, I strook forward against the Return of the Waves, and felt Ground again with my Feet. I stood still a few Moments to recover Breath, and till the Water went from me, and then took to my Heels, and run with

what Strength I had farther towards the Shore. But neither would this deliver me from the Fury of the Sea,
which came pouring in after me again, and twice more
I was lifted up by the Waves, and carried forwards as
before, the shore being very flat.

The last Time of these two had well near been fatal to
me; the Sea having hurried me along as before, landed
me, rather dash'd me against a Piece of a Rock, and that
with such Force, as it left me senseless, and indeed helpless, as my own Deliverance; for the Blow taking my Side
and breast, beat the Breath as it were quite out of my
Body; and it returned again immediately, I must have
been strangled in the Water; but I recover'd a little before

Illustration of Robinson Crusoe surviving the waves by clinging onto a rock.

the turn of the Waves, and seeing I should be cover'd again with the Water, I resolv'd to hold fast by a Piece of the Rock, and so to hold my Breath, if possible, till the Wave went back; now as the Waves were not so high as at first, being nearer Land, I held my Hold till the Wave abated, and then fetch'd another Run, which brought me so near the Shore, that the next Wave, tho' it went over me, yet did not so swallow me up as to carry me away, and the next run I took, I got to the main Land, where, to my great Comfort, I clamber'd up the Clifts of the Shore, and sat me down upon the Grass, free from Danger, and quite out of the Reach of the Water.

From **Robinson Crusoe**
by Daniel Defoe, 1719

Gulliver arrives in Lilliput

The character Gulliver, like Robinson Crusoe, has been shipwrecked on a desert island. The author, Jonathan Swift, liked to use fantastical stories to comment on the foolishness of society.

I was extremely tired, and with that, and the heat of the weather, and about half a pint of brandy that I drank as I left the ship, I found myself much inclined to sleep. I lay down on the grass, which was very short and soft, where I slept sounder than ever I remembered to have done in my life, and, as I reckoned, above nine hours; for when I awaked, it was just day-light. I attempted to rise, but was not able to stir: for, as I happened to lie on my back, I found my arms and legs were strongly fastened on each side to the ground; and my hair, which was long and thick, tied down in the same manner. I likewise felt several slender **ligatures** across my body, from my arm-pits to my thighs. I could only look upwards; the sun began to grow hot, and the light offended my eyes. I heard a confused noise about me; but in the posture I lay, could see nothing except the sky.

In a little time I felt something alive moving on my left leg, which advancing gently forward over my breast, came almost up to my chin; when, bending my eyes downwards as much as I could, I perceived it to be a human creature not six inches high, with a bow and arrow in his hands, and a quiver at his back. In the mean time, I felt at least forty more of the same kind (as I con- jectured) following the first. I was in the utmost aston- ishment, and roared so loud, that they all ran back in a fright; and some of them, as I was afterwards told, were hurt with the falls they got by leaping from my sides upon the ground. However, they soon returned, and one of them, who ventured so far as to get a full sight of my face, lifting up his hands and eyes by way of admir- ation, cried out in a shrill but distinct voice, *Hekinah Degul*: the others repeated the same words several times, but I then knew not what they meant.

I lay all this while, as the reader may believe, in great uneasiness. At length, struggling to get loose, I had the fortune to break the strings, and wrench out the pegs that fastened my left arm to the ground; for, by lifting it up to my face, I discovered the methods they had taken to bind me, and at the same time with a violent pull, which gave me excessive pain, I a little loosened the strings that tied down my hair on the left side, so that I was just able to turn my head about two inches.

But the creatures ran off a second time, before I could seize them; whereupon there was a great shout in a very shrill accent, and after it ceased I heard one of them cry aloud *Tolgo phonac;* when in an instant I felt above a hundred arrows discharged on my left hand, which, pricked me like so many needles; and besides, they shot another flight into the air, as we do bombs in Europe, whereof many, I suppose, fell on my body, (though I felt them not), and some on my face, which I immediately covered with my left hand. When this shower of arrows was over, I fell a groaning with grief and pain; and then striving again to get loose, they discharged another volley larger than the first, and some of them attempted with spears to stick me in the sides; but by good luck I had on me a **buff jerkin**, which they could not pierce.

I thought it the most prudent method to lie still, and my design was to continue so till night, when, my left hand being already loose, I could easily free myself: and as for the inhabitants, I had reason to believe I might be a match for the greatest army they could bring against me, if they were all of the same size with him that I saw. But fortune disposed otherwise of me. When the people observed I was quiet, they discharged no more arrows; but, by the noise I heard, I knew their numbers increased; and about four yards from me, over against my right ear, I heard a knocking for above an hour, like that of people at work; when turning my head that way, as well as the pegs and strings would permit me, I saw a stage erected about a foot and a half from the ground, capable of holding four of the inhabitants, with two or three ladders to mount it: from whence one of them, who seemed to be a person of quality, made me a long speech, whereof I understood not one syllable.

From **Gulliver's Travels** *by Jonathan Swift, 1726*

ligatures – ties, ropes
buff jerkin – leather jacket

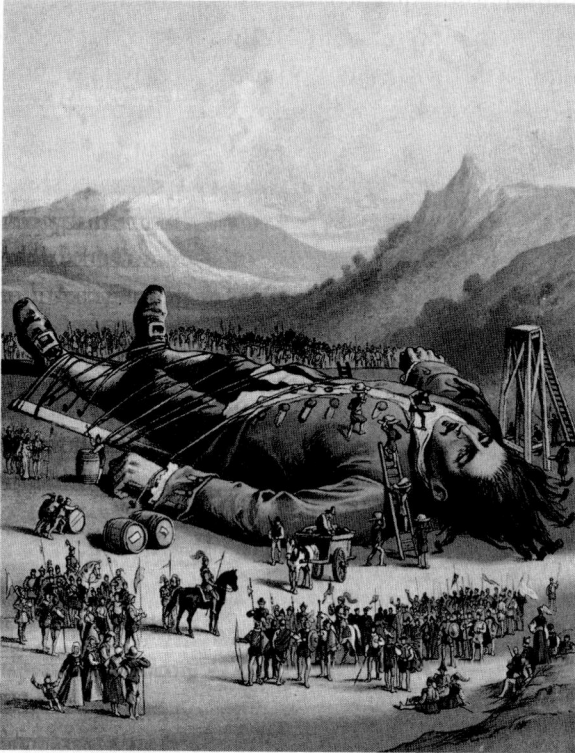

Illustration of Gulliver tied down in Lilliput.

Epigram

Alexander Pope, best known for his long poems and his translation of classic Roman literature, was also a master of writing witty rhyming couplets.

Engraved on the Collar of a Dog which I Gave to His Royal Highness

I am his Highness' Dog at Kew:
Pray tell me, sir, whose dog are you?

Alexander Pope, around 1730

Written on a window

This poem gives advice about the way to handle different people.

Tender-handed stroke a nettle
   And it stings you for your pains;
Grasp it like a man of **mettle**
   And it soft as silk remains.

'Tis the same with common natures:
   Use them kindly, they rebel;
But be rough as nutmeg-graters
   And the rogues obey you well.

Aaron Hill, around 1745

mettle – courage

The disabled soldier

The author Oliver Goldsmith one day met a man he knew when he was a boy. The man, dressed in a sailor's jacket and with a wooden leg, was begging in the street. The author was curious to know what had led him to be in this situation and so he asked the man for his life story.

'I went from town to town, worked when I could get employment, and starved when I could get none; when, happening one day to go through a field belonging to a justice of peace, I spied a hare crossing the path just before me; and I believe the devil put it into my head to fling my stick at it. Well, what will you have on't? I killed the hare, and was bringing it away, when the justice himself met me; he called me a poacher and a villain, and collaring me, desired I would give an account of myself. I fell upon my knees, begged his worship's pardon, and began to give a full account of all that I knew of my breed, seed, and generation; but though I gave a very true account, the justice said I could give no account; so I was indicted at the sessions, found guilty of being poor, and sent up to London to Newgate prison, in order to be **transported as a vagabond**.

'People may say this and that of being in jail, but, for my part, I found Newgate as agreeable a place as ever I was in all my life. I had my belly full to eat and drink, and did no work at all. This kind of life was too good to last for ever; so I was taken out of prison, after five months, put on board of ship, and sent off, with two hundred more, to the plantations. We had but an indifferent **passage**, for being all confined in the hold, more than a hundred of our people died for want of sweet air; and those that remained were sickly enough, God knows. When we came ashore we were sold to the planters, and I was bound for seven years more.

'When my time was expired, I worked my passage home, and glad I was to see old England again, because I loved my country. I was afraid, however, that I should be **indicted** for a vagabond once more, so did not much care to go down into the country, but kept about the town, and did little jobs when I could get them.

'I was very happy in this manner for some time till one evening, coming home from work, two men knocked me down, and then desired me to stand. They belonged to a **press-gang**. I was carried before the justice, and as I could give no account of myself, I had my choice left, whether to go on board a **man-of-war**, or list for a soldier. I chose the latter, and in this post of a gentleman, I served two campaigns in Flanders, was at the battles of Val and Fontenoy, and received but one wound through the breast here; but the doctor of our regiment soon made me well again ...

'But it was not my good fortune to have any promotion, for I soon fell sick, and so got leave to return home again with forty pounds in my pocket. This was at the beginning of the present war, and I hoped to be set on shore, and to have the pleasure of spending my money; but the Government wanted men, and so I was pressed for a sailor, before ever I could set a foot on shore.

'The boatswain found me, as he said, an obstinate fellow: he beat me without considering what he was about. I had still, however, my forty pounds, and that was some comfort to me under every beating; and the money I might have had to this day, but that our ship was taken by the French, and so I lost all.

'By good fortune we were retaken by the *Viper*. I had almost forgotten to tell you, that in that engagement, I was wounded in two places: I lost four fingers off the left hand, and my leg was shot off. If I had had the good fortune to have lost my leg and use of my hand on board a king's ship, and not aboard a **privateer**, I should have been entitled to clothing and maintenance during the rest of my life; but that was not my chance: one man is born with a silver spoon in his mouth, and another with a wooden ladle. However, blessed be God, I enjoy good health, and will for ever love liberty and old England. Liberty, property, and old England, for ever, huzza!'

From **The Disabled Soldier**
by Oliver Goldsmith, around 1760

transported as a vagabond – deported as a punishment
passage – journey by sea
indicted – convicted
press-gang – team which recruited new sailors by force
man-of-war – war ship
privateer – a merchant ship

Mrs Malaprop is offended by a letter

Mrs Malaprop is a character in Sheridan's comic play The Rivals. *She has a habit of using words in the wrong place. In this scene she reads out a love letter her daughter had received, not realising that she is reading it to the man who sent it, Captain Absolute ...*

MRS MALAPROP: Sir, you do me infinite honour! I beg, captain, you'll be seated. – [*They sit.*] Ah! few gentlemen, now-a-days, know how to value the ineffectual qualities in a woman! – few think how a little knowledge becomes a gentlewoman. – Men have no sense now but for the worthless flower of beauty!

ABSOLUTE: It is but too true, indeed, ma'am; – yet I fear our ladies should share the blame – they think our admiration of beauty so great, that knowledge in them would be superfluous. Thus, like garden-trees, they seldom show fruit, till time has robbed them of more specious blossom. – Few, like Mrs Malaprop and the orange-tree, are rich in both at once!

MRS MALAPROP: Sir, you overpower me with good-breeding. – He is the very pine-apple of politeness! – You are not ignorant, captain, that this giddy girl has somehow contrived to fix her affections on a beggarly, strolling, eaves-dropping ensign, whom none of us have seen, and nobody knows anything of.

ABSOLUTE: Oh, I have heard the silly affair before. – I'm not at all prejudiced against her on that account.

MRS MALAPROP: You are very good and very considerate, captain. I am sure I have done everything in my power since I exploded the affair; long ago I laid my positive conjunctions on her, never to think on the fellow again; – I have since laid Sir Anthony's preposition before her; but, I am sorry to say, she seems resolved to decline every particle that I enjoin her.

ABSOLUTE: It must be very distressing, indeed, ma'am.

Mrs Malaprop: Oh! it gives me the hydrostatics to such a degree. – I thought she had persisted from corresponding with him; but, behold, this very day, I have interceded another letter from the fellow; I believe I have it in my pocket.

Absolute: Oh, the devil! my last note.

[Aside]

Mrs Malaprop: Ay, here it is.

Absolute: Ay, my note indeed! Oh, the little traitress Lucy.

[Aside]

Mrs Malaprop: There, perhaps you may know the writing.

[Gives him the letter]

Absolute: I think I have seen the hand before – yes, I certainly must have seen this hand before –

Mrs Malaprop: Nay, but read it, captain.

Absolute: [Reads] *My soul's idol, my adored Lydia!* – Very tender, indeed!

Mrs Malaprop: Tender, ay, and profane too, o' my conscience.

Absolute: [Reads] *I am excessively alarmed at the intelligence you send me, the more so as my new rival–*

Mrs Malaprop: That's you, sir.

ABSOLUTE: [Reads] *Has universally the character of being an accomplished gentleman and a man of honour.* – Well, that's handsome enough.

MRS MALAPROP: Oh, the fellow has some design in writing so.

ABSOLUTE: That he had, I'll answer for him, ma'am.

MRS MALAPROP: But go on, sir – you'll see presently.

ABSOLUTE: [Reads] *As for the old weather-beaten she-dragon who guards you.* – Who can he mean by that?

MRS MALAPROP: Me, sir! – me! – he means me! – There – what do you think now? – but go on a little further.

ABSOLUTE: Impudent scoundrel! – [Reads] *it shall go hard but I will elude her vigilance, as I am told that the same ridiculous vanity, which makes her dress up her coarse features, and deck her dull chat with hard words which she don't understand*–

MRS MALAPROP: There, sir, an attack upon my language! what do you think of that? – an aspersion upon my parts of speech! was ever such a brute?! Sure, if I reprehend any thing in this world it is the use of my oracular tongue, and a nice derangement of epitaphs!

ABSOLUTE: He deserves to be hanged and quartered!

From **The Rivals** *by Richard Sheridan, 1775*

London

*This poem describes how grim and corrupt life had become
in the capital city at the time. Blake blamed the Church
and the State for oppressing people.*

I wander thro' each charter'd street,
Near where the charter'd Thames does flow,
And mark in every face I meet
Marks of weakness, marks of woe.

In every cry of every Man,
In every Infant's cry of fear,
In every voice, in every ban,
The mind-forg'd manacles I hear.

How the Chimney-sweeper's cry
Every black'ning Church appalls;
And the hapless Soldier's sigh
Runs in blood down Palace walls.

But most thro' midnight streets I hear
How the youthful Harlot's curse
Blasts the new-born Infant's tear,
And blights with plagues the Marriage hearse.

William Blake, 1794

William Blake's original illustrated page from *Songs of Innocence and Experience*.

The 1800s

The 1800s were a period of rapid change. The Industrial Revolution drew people away from the country to the big cities to find work in factories. They often lived on poor pay and in bad housing, with no help if they got sick or lost their jobs. But traders and manufacturers grew wealthier. The British Empire spread across the world.

At the same time, education reached more people, and girls from wealthy families were now taught to read and write. There was a great thirst for knowledge and improvement, plus a demand for reading material in newspapers and magazines.

Some of England's most famous novelists wrote in the 1800s – for example, Jane Austen, Charles Dickens and Charlotte Brontë. The first women writers were published, though some of them hid behind made-up male names.

The literature of this period explores personal feelings and relationships more deeply than ever before, but it also shows how society influences people and sometimes boxes them in.

Elizabeth upsets an important visitor

The love story in Jane Austen's novel Pride and Prejudice *between Elizabeth Bennet and Mr Darcy is said to be the love story on which all others are based. In this extract, Lady Catherine has come to see if the rumours are true that Elizabeth and Darcy are engaged, as she wants her own daughter to marry Darcy.*

'You can be at no loss, Miss Bennet, to understand the reason of my journey hither. Your own heart, your own conscience, must tell you why I come.'

Elizabeth looked with unaffected astonishment.

'Indeed, you are mistaken, Madam. I have not been at all able to account for the honour of seeing you here.'

'Miss Bennet,' replied her ladyship, in an angry tone, 'you ought to know, that I am not to be trifled with. But however insincere *you* may choose to be, you shall not find *me* so. My character has ever been celebrated for its sincerity and frankness, and in a cause of such moment as this, I shall certainly not depart from it. A report of a most alarming nature reached me two days ago. I was told that not only your sister was on the point of being most advantageously married, but that *you*, that Miss Elizabeth Bennet, would, in all likelihood, be soon afterwards united to my nephew, my own nephew, Mr Darcy. Though I *know* it must be a scandalous falsehood, though I would not injure him so much as to suppose the truth of it possible, I instantly resolved on setting off for this place, that I might make my sentiments known to you.'

'If you believed it impossible to be true,' said Elizabeth, colouring with astonishment and disdain, 'I wonder you took the trouble of coming so far. What could your ladyship propose by it?'

'At once to insist upon having such a report universally contradicted.'

'Your coming to Longbourn, to see me and my family,' said Elizabeth coolly, 'will be rather a confirmation of it; if, indeed, such a report is in existence.'

'If! Do you then pretend to be ignorant of it? Has it not been industriously circulated by yourselves? Do you not know that such a report is spread abroad?'

'I never heard that it was.'

'And can you likewise declare, that there is no *foundation* for it?'

'I do not pretend to possess equal frankness with your ladyship. *You* may ask questions which *I* shall not choose to answer.'

'This is not to be borne. Miss Bennet, I insist on being satisfied. Has he, has my nephew, made you an offer of marriage?'

'Your ladyship has declared it to be impossible...'

'I will not be interrupted. Hear me in silence. My daughter and my nephew are formed for each other. They are descended, on the maternal side, from the same noble line; and, on the father's, from respectable, honourable, and ancient – though untitled – families. Their fortune on both sides is splendid. They are destined for each other by the voice of every member of their respective houses; and what is to divide them? The upstart pretensions of a young woman without family, connections, or fortune. Is this to be endured! But it must not, shall not be. If you were sensible of your own good, you would not wish to quit the sphere in which you have been brought up.'

'In marrying your nephew, I should not consider myself as quitting that sphere. He is a gentleman; I am a gentleman's daughter; so far we are equal.'

'True. You *are* a gentleman's daughter. But who was your mother? Who are your uncles and aunts? Do not imagine me ignorant of their condition.'

'Whatever my connections may be,' said Elizabeth, 'if your nephew does not object to them, they can be nothing to *you*.'

'Tell me once for all, are you engaged to him?'

Portrait of Jane Austen.

Though Elizabeth would not, for the mere purpose of obliging Lady Catherine, have answered this question, she could not but say, after a moment's deliberation,

'I am not.'

Lady Catherine seemed pleased.

'And will you promise me, never to enter into such an engagement?'

'I will make no promise of the kind.'

'Miss Bennet I am shocked and astonished. I expected to find a more reasonable young woman. But do not deceive yourself into a belief that I will ever recede. I shall not go away till you have given me the assurance I require.'

'And I certainly *never* shall give it.'

From **Pride and Prejudice**
by Jane Austen, 1813

The murder of Nancy

When Dickens read this extract aloud to audiences, it is said that women wept and sometimes fainted. In this extract, the criminal Bill Sikes kills his lover, Nancy, in a fit of rage because he believes she has betrayed him to the police.

Without one pause, or moment's consideration; without once turning his head to the right or left, raising his eyes to the sky, or lowering them to the ground, but looking straight before him with savage resolution: his teeth so tightly compressed that the strained jaw seemed starting through his skin; the robber held on his headlong course, nor muttered a word, nor relaxed a muscle, until he reached his own door. He opened it, softly, with a key; strode lightly up the stairs; and entering his own room, doublelocked the door, and lifting a heavy table against it, drew back the curtain of the bed.

The girl was lying, half-dressed, upon it. He had roused her from her sleep, for she raised herself with a hurried and startled look.

'Get up!' said the man.

'It *is* you, Bill!' said the girl, with an expression of pleasure at his return.

'It is,' was the reply. 'Get up.'

There was a candle burning, but the man hastily drew it from the candlestick, and hurled it under the grate. Seeing the faint light of early day without, the girl rose to undraw the curtain.

'Let it be,' said Sikes, thrusting his hand before her. 'There's light enough for wot I've got to do.'

'Bill,' said the girl, in the low voice of alarm, 'why do you look like that at me!'

The robber sat regarding her, for a few seconds, with dilated nostrils and heaving breast; and then, grasping her by the head and throat, dragged her into the middle of the room, and looking once towards the door, placed his heavy hand upon her mouth.

'Bill, Bill!' gasped the girl, wrestling with the strength of mortal fear, – 'I – I – won't scream or cry – not once – hear me – speak to me – tell me what I have done!'

'You know, you she devil!' returned the robber, suppressing his breath. 'You were watched to-night; every word you said was heard.'

'Then spare my life for the love of Heaven, as I spared yours,' rejoined the girl, clinging to him. 'Bill, dear Bill, you cannot have the heart to kill me. Oh! think of all I have given up, only this one night, for you. You *shall* have time to think, and save yourself this crime; I will not loose my hold, you cannot throw me off. Bill, Bill, for dear God's sake, for your own, for mine, stop before you spill my blood! I have been true to you, upon my guilty soul I have!'

The man struggled violently, to release his arms; but those of the girl were clasped round his, and tear her as he would, he could not tear them away.

'Bill,' cried the girl, striving to lay her head upon his breast, 'the gentleman and that dear lady, told me to-night of a home in some foreign country where I could end my days in solitude and peace. Let me see them again, and beg them, on my knees, to show the same mercy and goodness to you; and let us both leave this dreadful place, and far apart lead better lives, and forget how we have lived, except in prayers, and never see each other more. It is never too late to repent. They told me so – I feel it now – but we must have time – a little, little time!'

The housebreaker freed one arm, and grasped his pistol. The certainty of immediate detection if he fired, flashed across his mind even in the midst of his fury; and he beat it twice with all the force he could summon, upon the upturned face that almost touched his own.

She staggered and fell: nearly blinded with the blood that rained down from a deep gash in her forehead, but raising herself, with difficulty, on her knees, drew from her bosom a white handkerchief – Rose Maylie's own – and holding it up, in her folded hands, as high towards Heaven as her feeble strength would allow, breathed one prayer for mercy to her Maker.

It was a ghastly figure to look upon. The murderer stag-gering backward to the wall, and shutting out the sight with his hand, seized a heavy club and struck her down.

Of all bad deeds that, under cover of the darkness, had been committed within wide London's bounds since night hung over it, that was the worst. Of all the horrors that rose with an ill scent upon the morning air, that was the foulest and most cruel.

The sun – the bright sun, that brings back, not light alone, but new life, and hope, and freshness to man – burst upon the crowded city in clear and radiant glory. Through costly-coloured glass and paper-mended window, through cathedral dome and rotten crevice, it shed its equal ray. It lighted up the room where the murdered woman lay. It did. He tried to shut it out, but it would stream in. If the sight had been a ghastly one in the dull morning, what was it, now, in all that brilliant light!

He had not moved; he had been afraid to stir. There had been a moan and motion of the hand; and, with terror added to rage, he had struck and struck again. Once he threw a rug over it; but it was worse to fancy the eyes, and imagine them moving towards him, than to see them glaring upward, as if watching the reflection of the pool of gore that quivered and danced in the sunlight on the ceiling. He had plucked it off again. And there was the body – mere flesh and blood, no more – but such flesh, and so much blood!

He struck a light, kindled a fire, and thrust the club into it. There was hair upon the end, which blazed and shrunk into a light cinder, and, caught by the air, whirled up the chimney. Even that frightened him, sturdy as he was; but he held the weapon till it broke, and then piled it on the coals to burn away, and smoulder into ashes. He washed himself, and rubbed his clothes; there were spots that would not be removed, but he cut the pieces out, and burnt them. How those stains were dispersed about the room! The very feet of the dog were bloody.

All this time he had, never once, turned his back upon the corpse; no, not for a moment. Such preparations completed, he moved, backward, towards the door: dragging the dog with him, lest he should soil his feet anew and carry out new evidences of the crime into the streets. He shut the door softly, locked it, took the key, and left the house.

From Oliver Twist
by Charles Dickens, 1838

Bill Sikes surveys the body of Nancy from David Lean's 1948 film adaptation of *Oliver Twist*.

I Am

John Clare wrote this poem in a mental asylum, where he spent his dying years.

I am: yet what I am none cares or knows,
My friends forsake me like a memory lost;
I am the self-consumer of my woes,
They rise and vanish in oblivious host,
Like shades in love and death's oblivion lost;
And yet I am! and live with shadows **tost**

Into the nothingness of scorn and noise,
Into the living sea of waking dreams,
Where there is neither sense of life nor joys,
But the vast shipwreck of my life's esteems;
And e'en the dearest – that I loved the best-
Are strange – nay, rather stranger than the rest.

I long for scenes where man has never trod;
A place where woman never smil'd or wept;
There to abide with my creator, God,
And sleep as I in childhood sweetly slept:
Untroubling and untroubled where I lie;
The grass below – above the vaulted sky.

John Clare, around 1845

tost – thrown

Jane Eyre is woken by a strange noise

This passage from Jane Eyre *by Charlotte Brontë describes an incident that occurs when she is living as a governess in Mr Rochester's house.*

I started wide awake on hearing a vague murmur, peculiar and lugubrious, which sounded, I thought, just above me. I wished I had kept my candle burning: the night was drearily dark; my spirits were depressed. I rose and sat up in bed, listening. The sound was hushed.

I tried again to sleep; but my heart beat anxiously: my inward tranquillity was broken. The clock, far down in the hall, struck two. Just then it seemed my chamber-door was touched; as if fingers had swept the panels in groping a way along the dark gallery outside. I said, 'Who is there?' Nothing answered. I was chilled with fear…

This was a demoniac laugh – low, suppressed, and deep – uttered, as it seemed, at the very keyhole of my chamber door. The head of my bed was near the door, and I thought at first the goblin-laugher stood at my bedside – or rather, crouched by my pillow: but I rose, looked round, and could see nothing; while, as I still gazed, the unnatural sound was reiterated: and I knew it came from behind the panels. My first impulse was to rise and fasten the bolt; my next, again to cry out, 'Who is there?'

Something gurgled and moaned. Ere long, steps retreated up the gallery towards the third-storey staircase: a door had lately been made to shut in that staircase; I heard it open and close, and all was still.

'Was that Grace Poole? and is she possessed with a devil?' thought I. Impossible now to remain longer by myself: I must go to Mrs Fairfax. I hurried on my frock and a shawl; I withdrew the bolt and opened the door with a trembling hand. There was a candle burning just outside, and on the matting in the gallery. I was surprised at this circumstance: but still more was I amazed to perceive the air quite dim, as if filled with smoke; and, while looking to the right hand and left, to find whence these blue wreaths issued, I became further aware of a strong smell of burning.

Something creaked: it was a door ajar; and that door was Mr Rochester's, and the smoke rushed in a cloud from thence. I thought no more of Mrs Fairfax; I thought no more of Grace Poole, or the laugh: in an instant, I was within the chamber. Tongues of flame darted round the bed: the curtains were on fire. In the midst of blaze and vapour, Mr Rochester lay stretched motionless, in deep sleep.

'Wake! wake!' I cried. I shook him, but he only murmured and turned: the smoke had stupefied him. Not a moment could be lost: the very sheets were kindling, I rushed to his basin and ewer; fortunately, one was wide and the other deep, and both were filled with water. I heaved them up, deluged the bed and its occupant, flew back to my own room, brought my own water-jug, baptized the couch afresh, and, by God's aid, succeeded in extinguishing the flames which were devouring it.

The hiss of the quenched element, the breakage of a pitcher which I flung from my hand when I had emptied it, and, above all, the splash of the shower-bath I had liberally bestowed, roused Mr Rochester at last. Though it was now dark, I knew he was awake; because I heard him **fulminating** strange **anathemas** at finding himself lying in a pool of water.

'Is there a flood?' he cried.

'No, sir,' I answered; 'but there has been a fire.'

From **Jane Eyre**
by Charlotte Brontë, 1847

fulminating – raging
anathemas – swear words

A pause

This is a poem about the moment between life and death.

They made the chamber sweet with flowers and
   leaves,
   And the bed sweet with flowers on which I lay;
   While my soul, love-bound, loitered on its way.
I did not hear the birds about the eaves,
Nor hear the reapers talk among the sheaves:
   Only my soul kept watch from day to day,
   My thirsty soul kept watch for one away: –
Perhaps he loves, I thought, remembers, grieves.
At length there came the step upon the stair,
   Upon the lock the old familiar hand:
Then first my spirit seemed to scent the air
   Of Paradise; then first the tardy sand
Of time ran golden; and I felt my hair
Put on a glory, and my soul expand.

Christina Rossetti, around 1860

The charge of the light brigade

This poem was written about a disastrous cavalry charge led by Lord Cardigan during the Battle of Balaclava in the Crimean War. Many of the men were killed or wounded and did not return home.

1.
Half a league, half a league,
   Half a league onward,
All in the valley of Death
   Rode the six hundred.

'Forward, the Light Brigade!'
'Charge for the guns!' he said:
Into the valley of Death
    Rode the six hundred.

2.
'Forward, the Light Brigade!'
Was there a man dismay'd?
Not tho' the soldier knew
    Someone had blunder'd:
Their's not to make reply,
Their's not to reason why,
Their's but to do and die:
Into the valley of Death
    Rode the six hundred.

3.
Cannon to right of them,
Cannon to left of them,
Cannon in front of them
    Volley'd and thunder'd;
Storm'd at with shot and shell,
Boldly they rode and well,
Into the jaws of Death,
Into the mouth of Hell
    Rode the six hundred.

4.
Flash'd all their sabres bare,
Flash'd as they turn'd in air,
Sabring the gunners there,
Charging an army, while
    All the world wonder'd:

Plunged in the battery-smoke
Right thro' the line they broke;
Cossack and Russian
Reel'd from the sabre stroke
   Shatter'd and sunder'd.
Then they rode back, but not
   Not the six hundred.

5.
Cannon to right of them,
Cannon to left of them,
Cannon behind them
   Volley'd and thunder'd;
Storm'd at with shot and shell,
While horse and hero fell,
They that had fought so well
Came thro' the jaws of Death
Back from the mouth of Hell,
All that was left of them,
   Left of six hundred.

6.
When can their glory fade?
O the wild charge they made!
   All the world wondered.
Honour the charge they made,
Honour the Light Brigade,
   Noble six hundred!

Alfred, Lord Tennyson, 1854

Engraving of the "Charge of the Light Brigade" during the Crimean War.

Heaven-haven
A nun takes the veil

This woman looks forward to a new life of total peace on the day she becomes a nun and withdraws from life outside.

I have desired to go
Where springs not fail,
To fields where flies no sharp and sided hail
And a few lilies blow.

And I have asked to be
Where no storms come
Where the green swell is in the **havens dumb**
And out of the swing of the sea

Gerard Manley Hopkins, 1866

havens dumb – quiet seas in the harbour

A drunken man sells his wife

This extract is from the first chapter of a novel written by Thomas Hardy. A traveller has stopped at a beer tent with his wife and baby and is getting increasingly drunk.

At the end of the first **basin** the man had risen to serenity; at the second he was jovial; at the third, argumentative; at the fourth, the qualities signified by the shape of his face, the occasional clench of his mouth, and the fiery spark of his dark eye, began to tell in his conduct; he was overbearing – even brilliantly quarrelsome.

The conversation took a high turn, as it often does on such occasion. The ruin of good men by bad wives,

60

and the frustration of high aims and hopes was the theme.

'I did for myself that way thoroughly,' said the **trusser**, with a contemplative bitterness that was well-nigh resentful. 'I married at eighteen, like the fool that I was; and this is the consequence o't.' He pointed at himself and family with a wave of the hand.

The young woman his wife, who seemed accustomed to such remarks, acted as if she did not hear them, and continued her intermittent private words on tender trifles to the sleeping and waking child, who was just big enough to be placed for a moment on the bench beside her when she wished to ease her arms. The man continued–

'I haven't more than fifteen shillings in the world, and yet I am a good experienced hand in my line. I'd challenge England to beat me in the **fodder** business; and if I were a free man again I'd be worth a thousand pound before I'd done o't. But a fellow never knows these little things till all chance of acting upon 'em is past.'

The auctioneer selling the old horses in the field outside could he heard saying, 'Now this is the last lot – now who'll take the last lot for a song? Shall I say forty shillings? 'Tis a very promising **brood-mare**, a trifle over five years old, and nothing the matter with the hoss at all, except that she's a little **holler** in the back and had her left eye knocked out by the kick of another, her own sister, coming along the road.'

'For my part I don't see why men who have got wives and don't want 'em shouldn't get rid of 'em as these gipsy fellows do their old horses,' said the man in the tent. 'Why shouldn't they put 'em up and sell 'em by auction to men who are in need of such articles? Hey?

Why, begad, I'd sell mine this minute if anybody would buy her!'

'There's them that would do that,' some of the guests replied, looking at the woman, who was by no means ill-favoured.

'I know I've said it before; I meant it. All I want is a buyer.'

At that moment a swallow, one among the last of the season, which had by chance found its way through an opening into the upper part of the tent, flew to and fro in quick curves above their heads, causing all eyes to follow it absently. In watching the bird till it made its escape the assembled company neglected to respond to the workman's offer, and the subject dropped.

But a quarter of an hour later the man, who had gone on lacing his **furmity** more and more heavily, though he was either so strong-minded or such an intrepid toper that he still appeared fairly sober, recurred to the old strain, as in a musical fantasy the instrument fetches up the original theme. 'Here – I am waiting to know about this offer of mine. The woman is no good to me. Who'll have her?'

The company had by this time decidedly degenerated, and the renewed inquiry was received with a laugh of appreciation. The woman whispered; she was imploring and anxious: 'Come, come, it is getting dark, and this nonsense won't do. If you don't come along, I shall go without you. Come!'

She waited and waited; yet he did not move. In ten minutes the man broke in upon the desultory conversation of the furmity drinkers with, 'I asked this question, and nobody answered to 't. Will any Jack Rag or Tom Straw among ye buy my goods?'

The woman's manner changed, and her face assumed the grim shape and colour of which mention has been made.

'Mike, Mike,' said she; 'this is getting serious. O! – too serious!'

'Will anybody buy her?' said the man.

'I wish somebody would,' said she firmly. 'Her present owner is not at all to her liking!'

'Nor you to mine,' said he. 'So we are agreed about that. Gentlemen, you hear? It's an agreement to part. She shall take the girl if she wants to, and go her ways. I'll take my tools, and go my ways. 'Tis simple as Scripture history. Now then, stand up, Susan, and show yourself.'

'Don't, my **chiel**,' whispered a buxom **staylace** dealer in voluminous petticoats, who sat near the woman; 'yer good man don't know what he's saying.'

The woman, however, did stand up. 'Now, who's auctioneer?' cried the hay-trusser.

'I be,' promptly answered a short man, with a nose resembling a copper knob, a damp voice, and eyes like buttonholes. 'Who'll make an offer for this lady?'

The woman looked on the ground, as if she maintained her position by a supreme effort of will.

'Five shillings,' said some one, at which there was a laugh.

'No insults,' said the husband. 'Who'll say a guinea?'

Nobody answered; and the female dealer in staylaces interposed.

'Behave yerself **moral**, good man, for Heaven's love! Ah, what a cruelty is the poor soul married to! Bed and board is dear at some figures, 'pon my **'vation** 'tis!'

'Set it higher, auctioneer,' said the trusser.

'Two guineas!' said the auctioneer; and no one replied.

'If they don't take her for that, in ten seconds they'll have to give more,' said the husband. 'Very well. Now, auctioneer, add another.'

'Three guineas – going for three guineas!' said the rheumy man.

'No bid?' said the husband. 'Good Lord, why she's cost me fifty times the money, if a penny. Go on.'

'Four guineas!' cried the auctioneer.

'I'll tell ye what – I won't sell her for less than five,' said the husband, bringing down his fist so that the basins danced. 'I'll sell her for five guineas to any man that will pay me the money, and treat her well; and he shall have her for ever, and never hear aught o' me. But she shan't go for less. Now then – five guineas – and she's yours. Susan, you agree?'

She bowed her head with absolute indifference.

'Five guineas,' said the auctioneer, 'or she'll be withdrawn. Do anybody give it? The last time. Yes or no?'

'Yes,' said a loud voice from the doorway.

All eyes were turned. Standing in the triangular opening which formed the door of the tent was a sailor, who, unobserved by the rest, had arrived there within the last two or three minutes. A dead silence followed his affirmation.

'You say you do?' asked the husband, staring at him.

'I say so,' replied the sailor.

From **The Mayor of Casterbridge**
by Thomas Hardy, 1886

basin – cooking pot	**furmity** – an alcoholic dish
trusser – farm worker	**chiel** – child
fodder – animal feed	**staylace** – corset
brood-mare – horse for breeding	**moral** – properly, doing what's right
holler – arched, drooping	**'vation** – salvation

The 1900s

The first half of the 1900s was dominated by two world wars, which had an enormous impact on society and the way writers saw the world. The First World War was an ugly war in which millions died. Ordinary soldiers came home from the trenches wanting a better world and an improved standard of living. They did not trust the upper class to run society as they had done before. Women voted for the first time. The Labour Party became a new force in British politics. The British Empire was broken up and new world powers emerged.

New technology in the second half of the century brought many changes to the way we work. Women's vote, education for all, the mass media, air travel, the computer and the Internet transformed everyday life. Everyone was entitled to go to school and stayed in education for longer, so most people learned to read and write well enough to read a newspaper, enjoy a novel or write a story. The voices and experiences of ordinary working people were now heard in literature, and more women than ever before became writers. Literature expanded into new media such as television, radio and Internet.

The literature of the twentieth century moved from polite Victorian prose to angry plays, unusual poetry and disturbing novels. It is often said of the twentieth century that people lost their belief in God, and could no longer see much meaning in life.

Teaching a common flower-seller to speak in standard English

This play was transformed into the popular musical **My Fair Lady.** *The writer, George Bernard Shaw, was a well-known socialist, and one of his writing habits was to ignore certain apostrophes (').*

PICKERING [*gently*]: What is it you want, my girl?

THE FLOWER GIRL: I want to be a lady in a flower shop stead of selling at the corner of Tottenham Court Road. But they wont take me unless I can talk more genteel. He said he could teach me. Well, here I am ready to pay him – not asking any favour – and he treats me as if I was dirt.

MRS PEARCE: How can you be such a foolish ignorant girl as to think you could afford to pay Mr Higgins?

THE FLOWER GIRL: Why shouldnt I? I know what lessons cost as well as you do; and I'm ready to pay.

HIGGINS: How much?

THE FLOWER GIRL [*coming back to him, triumphant*]: Now youre talking! I thought youd come off it when you saw a chance of getting back a bit of what you chucked at me last night. [*Confidentially*] Youd had a drop in, hadnt you?

HIGGINS [*peremptorily*]: Sit down.

THE FLOWER GIRL: Oh, if youre going to make a compliment of it–

HIGGINS [*thundering at her*]: Sit down.

MRS PEARCE [*severely*]: Sit down, girl. Do as youre told. [*She places the stray chair near the hearthrug between Higgins and Pickering, and stands behind it waiting for the girl to sit down.*]

THE FLOWER GIRL: Ah-ah-ah-ow-ow-oo! [*She stands, half rebellious, half bewildered.*]

PICKERING [*very courteous*]: Wont you sit down?

LIZA [*coyly*]: Don't mind if I do. [*She sits down. Pickering returns to the hearthrug.*]

HIGGINS: Whats your name?

THE FLOWER GIRL: Liza Doolittle.

HIGGINS [*declaiming gravely*]: Eliza, Elizabeth, Betsy and Bess, They went to the woods to get a bird nes':

PICKERING: They found a nest with four egg in it:

HIGGINS: They took one apiece, and left three in it.

They laugh heartily at their own wit.

LIZA: Oh, don't be silly.

MRS PEARCE: You mustnt speak to the gentleman like that.

LIZA: Well, why wont he speak sensible to me?

HIGGINS: Come back to business. How much do you propose to pay me for the lessons?

LIZA: Oh, I know whats right. A lady friend of mine gets French lessons for eighteenpence an hour from a real French gentleman. Well, you wouldnt have the face to ask me the same for teaching me my own language as you would for French; so I wont give more than a shilling. Take it or leave it.

HIGGINS [*walking up and down the room, rattling his keys and his cash in his pockets*]: You know, Pickering, if you consider a shilling, not as a simple shilling, but as a percentage of this girl's income, it works out as fully equivalent to sixty or seventy guineas from a millionaire.

PICKERING: How so?

HIGGINS: Figure it out. A millionaire has about £150 a day. She earns about half-a-crown.

LIZA [*haughtily*]: Who told you I only—

HIGGINS [*continuing*]: She offers me two-fifths of her day's income for a lesson. Two-fifths of a millionaire's income for a day would be somewhere about £60. It's handsome. By George, it's enormous! it's the biggest offer I ever had.

LIZA [*rising, terrified*]: Sixty pounds! What are you talking about? I never offered you sixty pounds. Where would I get—

HIGGINS: Hold your tongue.

LIZA [*weeping*]: But I aint got sixty pounds. Oh—

MRS PEARCE: Don't cry, you silly girl. Sit down. Nobody is going to touch your money.

HIGGINS: Somebody is going to touch you, with a broomstick, if you dont stop snivelling. Sit down.

LIZA [*obeying slowly*]: Ah-ah-ah-ow-oo-o! One would think you was my father.

HIGGINS: If I decide to teach you, I'll be worse than two fathers to you. Here [*he offers her his silk handkerchief*]!

LIZA: Whats this for?

HIGGINS: To wipe your eyes. To wipe any part of your face that feels moist. Remember: thats your handkerchief; and thats your sleeve. Dont mistake the one for the other if you wish to become a lady in a shop.

Liza, utterly bewildered, stares helplessly at him.

MRS PEARCE: It's no use talking to her like that, Mr Higgins: she doesnt understand you. Besides, youre quite wrong: she doesnt do it that way at all [*she takes the handkerchief*].

LIZA [*snatching it*]: Here! You give me that handkerchief. He give it to me, not to you.

PICKERING [*laughing*]: He did. I think it must be regarded as her property, Mrs Pearce.

MRS PEARCE [*resigning herself*]: Serve you right, Mr Higgins.

PICKERING: Higgins: I'm interested. What about the ambassador's garden party? I'll say youre the greatest teacher alive if you make that good. I'll bet you all the expenses of the experiment you cant do it. And I'll pay for the lessons.

LIZA: Oh, you are real good. Thank you, Captain.

HIGGINS [*tempted, looking at her*]: It's almost irresistible. Shes so deliciously low – so horribly dirty–

LIZA [*protesting extremely*]: Ah-ah-ah-ah-ow-ow-oo-oo!!! I aint dirty: I washed my face and hands afore I come, I did.

PICKERING: Youre certainly not going to turn her head with flattery, Higgins.

MRS PEARCE [*uneasy*]: Oh, dont say that, sir: theres more ways than one of turning a girl's head; and nobody can do it better than Mr Higgins, though he may not always mean it. I do hope, sir, you wont encourage him to do anything foolish.

HIGGINS [*becoming excited as the idea grows on him*]: What is life but a series of inspired follies? The difficulty is to find them to do. Never lose a chance: it doesnt come every day. I shall make a duchess of this draggle-tailed guttersnipe.

LIZA [*strongly deprecating this view of her*]: Ah-ah-ah-ow-ow-oo!

HIGGINS [*carried away*]: Yes: in six months – in three if she has a good ear and a quick tongue – I'll take her anywhere and pass her off as anything. We'll start today: now! this moment! Take her away and clean her, Mrs Pearce.

From **Pygmalion**
by George Bernard Shaw, 1912

Scene from *My Fair Lady* with Audrey Hepburn as Eliza Doolittle – a musical retelling of *Pygmalion*.

These I have loved

This poem was written by Rupert Brooke, a well-known poet who died shortly afterwards in the First World War.

These I have loved:
White plates and cups, clean-gleaming,
Ringed with blue lines; and feathery, faery dust;
Wet roofs, beneath the lamp-light; the strong crust
Of friendly bread; and many-tasting food;
Rainbows; and the blue bitter smoke of wood;
And radiant raindrops couching in cool flowers;
And flowers themselves, that sway through sunny
  hours,
Dreaming of moths that drink them under the
  moon;
Then, the cool kindliness of sheets, that soon
Smooth away trouble; and the rough male kiss
Of blankets; grainy wood; live hair that is
Shining and free; blue-massing clouds; the keen
Unpassioned beauty of a great machine;
The **benison** of hot water; furs to touch;
The good smell of old clothes; and other such –

From 'The Great Lover'
by Rupert Brooke, 1914

benison – blessing

Cargoes

John Masefield was poet laureate from 1930 until his death in 1967. He wrote poems, plays and novels. This poem compares the colourful past with the dreary present.

Quinquireme of Nineveh from distant Ophir
Rowing home to haven in sunny Palestine,
With a cargo of ivory,
And apes and peacocks,
Sandalwood, cedarwood, and sweet white wine.

Stately Spanish galleon coming from the **Isthmus**,
Dipping through the Tropics by the palm-green shores,
With a cargo of diamonds,
Emeralds, amethysts,
Topazes, and cinnamon, and gold **moidores**.

Dirty British coaster with a salt-caked smoke stack
Butting through the Channel in the mad March days,
With a cargo of Tyne coal,
Road-rails, **pig-lead**,
Firewood, iron-ware, and cheap tin trays.

John Masefield, 1917

quinquireme – ancient warship powered by oars
Isthmus – narrow strip of land between two seas
moidores – gold coins
pig-lead – crude lead cast in big blocks

Dulce et decorum est

*This poem is one of Wilfred Owen's best-known works.
It describes a gas attack in the trenches of the First World
War – something Owen experienced first-hand. He was
killed on the last day of the war.*

Bent double, like old beggars under sacks,
Knock-kneed, coughing like hags, we cursed through
    sludge,

73

Till on the haunting flares we turned our backs
And towards our distant rest began to trudge.
Men marched asleep. Many had lost their boots
But limped on, blood-shod. All went lame; all blind;
Drunk with fatigue; deaf even to the hoots
Of gas shells dropping softly behind.

Gas! GAS! Quick, boys! – An ecstasy of fumbling,
Fitting the clumsy helmets just in time;
But someone still was yelling out and stumbling
And floundering like a man in fire or lime. –
Dim, through the misty panes and thick green light
As under a green sea, I saw him drowning.

In all my dreams, before my helpless sight,
He plunges at me, guttering, choking, drowning.

If in some smothering dreams you too could pace
Behind the wagon that we flung him in,
And watch the white eyes writhing in his face,
His hanging face, like a devil's sick of sin;
If you could hear, at every jolt, the blood
Come gargling from the froth-corrupted lungs,
Obscene as cancer, bitter as the cud
Of vile, incurable sores on innocent tongues, –
My friend, you would not tell with such high zest
To children ardent for some desperate glory,
The old Lie: **Dulce et decorum est
Pro patria mori**.

Wilfred Owen, 1918

Dulce et decorum est pro patria mori – it is right and proper to die for your country

Wilfred Owen's hand-written original of *Dulce et decorum est.*

The Hollow Men

The voices in this poem speak about their experience of death. However, some readers think that it also shows the way Eliot saw people in the modern world as living empty pointless lives, like living dead.

I
We are the hollow men
We are the stuffed men

Leaning together
Headpiece filled with straw. Alas!
Our dried voices, when
We whisper together
Are quiet and meaningless
As wind in dry grass
Or rats' feet over broken glass
In our dry cellar

Shape without form, shade without colour,
Paralysed force, gesture without motion;

Those who have crossed
With direct eyes, to death's other Kingdom
Remember us – if at all – not as lost
Violent souls, but only
As the hollow men
The stuffed men.

II
Eyes I dare not meet in dreams
In death's dream kingdom
These do not appear:
There, the eyes are
Sunlight on a broken column
There, is a tree swinging
And voices are
In the wind's singing
More distant and more solemn
Than a fading star.

Let me be no nearer
In death's dream kingdom
Let me also wear

Such deliberate disguises
Rat's coat, crowskin, crossed staves
In a field
Behaving as the wind behaves
No nearer —

Not that final meeting
In the twilight kingdom

III
This is the dead land
This is cactus land
Here the stone images
Are raised, here they receive
The supplication of a dead man's hand
Under the twinkle of a fading star.

Is it like this
In death's other kingdom
Waking alone
At the hour when we are
Trembling with tenderness
Lips that would kiss
Form prayers to broken stone.

★★★★★

This is the way the world ends
This is the way the world ends
This is the way the world ends
Not with a bang but a whimper.

From '**The Hollow Men**'
by T. S. Eliot, 1925

New arrivals from England

The writer Doris Lessing moved to Africa when she was a child, and lived there for twenty-five years. This experience inspired much of her work, including the short story from which this extract is taken.

There, outside the front door, was a car, an ancient **jalopy** bulging with luggage, its back doors tied with rope. And children! She could see a half-brown girl on the steps. No, really, it was too much. On the other side of the car stooped a tall, thin, fairheaded man, burnt as brown as toffee, looking for someone to come. He must be the father. She approached, adjusting her face to a smile, looking apprehensively about her for the children. The man slowly came forward, the girl after him. 'I expected you earlier,' began Mrs Gale briskly, looking reproachfully into the man's face. His eyes were cautious, blue, assessing. He looked her casually up and down and seemed not to take her into account. 'Is Major Gale about?' he asked. 'I am Mrs Gale,' she replied. Then, again: 'I expected you earlier.' Really, four hours late and not a word of apology!

'We started late,' he remarked. 'Where can I put our things?' Mrs Gale swallowed her annoyance and said: 'I didn't know you had a family. I didn't make arrangements.'

'I wrote to the Major about my wife,' said De Wet. 'Didn't he get my letter?' He sounded offended.

Weakly Mrs Gale said: 'Your wife?' and looked in wonderment at the girl, who was smiling awkwardly behind her husband. It could be seen, looking at her more closely, that she might perhaps be eighteen. She was a small creature, with delicate brown legs and arms, a brush of dancing black curls, and large excited black eyes. She put both hands round her husband's arm, and said, giggling: 'I am Mrs De Wet.'

De Wet put her away from him, gently, but so that she pouted and said: 'We got married last week.'

'Last week,' said Mrs Gale, conscious of dislike.

The girl said, with an extraordinary mixture of effrontery and shyness: 'He met me in a cinema and we got married next day.' It seemed as if she were in some way offering herself to the older woman, offering something precious of herself.

'Really,' said Mrs Gale politely, glancing almost apprehensively at this man, this slow-moving, **laconic**, shrewd South African, who had behaved with such violence and folly. Distaste twisted her again.

Suddenly the man said, grasping the girl by the arm, and gently shaking her to and fro, in a sort of controlled exasperation: 'Thought I had better get myself a wife to cook for me, all this way out in the blue. No restaurants here, hey, Doodle?'

'Oh, Jack,' pouted the girl, giggling. 'All he thinks about is his stomach,' she said to Mrs Gale, as one girl to another, and then glanced with delicious fear up at her husband.

'Cooking is what I married you for,' he said, smiling down at her intimately.

There stood Mrs Gale opposite them, and she saw that they had forgotten her existence; and that it was only by the greatest effort of will that they did not kiss. 'Well,' she remarked drily, 'this is a surprise.'

They fell apart, their faces changing. They became at once what they had been during the first moments: two hostile strangers. They looked at her across the barrier that seemed to shut the world away from them. They saw a middle-aged English lady, in a shapeless old-fashioned blue silk dress, with a gold locket sliding over a flat bosom, smiling at them coldly, her blue, misted eyes critically narrowed.

From **The De Wets Come to Kloof Grange**
by Doris Lessing, 1951

jalopy – car
laconic – uncommunicative, quiet

Waiting for Godot

Samuel Beckett is a writer well-known for plays that express a sense of loss and meaninglessness.

VLADIMIR: You're a hard man to get on with, Gogo.

ESTRAGON: It'd be better if we parted.

VLADIMIR: You always say that, and you always come crawling back.

ESTRAGON: The best thing would be to kill me, like the other.

VLADIMIR: What other? *(Pause.)* What other?

ESTRAGON: Like billions of others.

VLADIMIR *(sententious):* To every man his little cross. *(He sighs.)* Till he dies. *(Afterthought.)* And is forgotten.

ESTRAGON: In the meantime let us try and converse calmly, since we are incapable of keeping silent.

VLADIMIR: You're right, we're inexhaustible.

ESTRAGON: It's so we won't think.

VLADIMIR: We have that excuse.

ESTRAGON: It's so we won't hear.

VLADIMIR: We have our reasons.

ESTRAGON: All the dead voices.

VLADIMIR: They make a noise like wings.

ESTRAGON: Like leaves.

VLADIMIR: Like sand.

ESTRAGON: Like leaves.

Silence.

VLADIMIR: They all speak together.

ESTRAGON: Each one to itself.

Silence.

VLADIMIR: Rather they whisper.

ESTRAGON: They rustle.

VLADIMIR: They murmur.

ESTRAGON: They rustle.

Silence.

VLADIMIR: What do they say?

ESTRAGON: They talk about their lives.

VLADIMIR: To have lived is not enough for them.

ESTRAGON: They have to talk about it.

VLADIMIR: To be dead is not enough for them.

ESTRAGON: It is not sufficient.

Silence.

VLADIMIR: They make noise like feathers.

ESTRAGON: Like leaves.

VLADIMIR: Like ashes.

ESTRAGON: Like leaves.

Long silence.

VLADIMIR: Say something!

ESTRAGON: I'm trying.

Long silence.

VLADIMIR (*in anguish*): Say anything at all!

ESTRAGON: What do we do now?

VLADIMIR: Wait for Godot.

ESTRAGON: Ah!

Silence.

From **Waiting for Godot**
by Samuel Beckett, 1952

sententious – very moral

Breakdown

Sylvia Plath was a poet as well as a novelist, and her most common theme was the experience of being a woman. She had a feel for the stress and emptiness often felt by young and able women in a world that expected them to be wives and mothers rather than equals to men. She committed suicide in 1963, after suffering from severe depression.

I followed Doctor Gordon. A door opened somewhere in the distance, and I heard a woman shouting.

All at once a nurse popped around the corner of the corridor ahead of us leading a woman in a blue bathrobe with shaggy, waist-length hair. Doctor Gordon stepped back, and I flattened against the wall.

As the woman was dragged by, waving her arms and struggling in the grip of the nurse, she was saying, 'I'm going to jump out of the window, I'm going to jump out of the window, I'm going to jump out of the window.'

Dumpy and muscular in her smudge-fronted uniform, the wall-eyed nurse wore such thick spectacles that four eyes peered out at me from behind the round, twin panes of glass. I was trying to tell which eyes were the real eyes and which the false eyes, and which of the real eyes was the wall-eye and which the straight eye, when she brought her face up to mine with a large, conspiratorial grin and hissed, as if to reassure me, 'She thinks she's going to jump out the window but she can't jump out the window because they're all barred!'

And as Doctor Gordon led me into a bare room at the back of the house, I saw that the windows in that part were indeed barred, and that the room door and the closet door and the drawers of the bureau and everything that opened and shut was fitted with a keyhole so it could be locked up.

I lay down on the bed.

The wall-eyed nurse came back. She unclasped my watch and dropped it in her pocket. Then she started tweaking the hairpins from my hair.

Doctor Gordon was unlocking the closet. He dragged out a table of wheels with a machine on it and rolled it behind the head of the bed. The nurse started swabbing my temples with a smelly grease.

As she leaned over to reach the side of my head nearest the wall, her fat breast muffled my face like a cloud or a pillow. A vague, medicinal stench emanated from her flesh.

'Don't worry,' the nurse grinned down at me. 'Their first time everybody's scared to death.'

I tried to smile, but my skin had gone stiff, like parchment.

Doctor Gordon was fitting two metal plates on either side of my head. He buckled them into place with a strap that dented my forehead, and gave me a wire to bite.

I shut my eyes.

There was a brief silence, like an indrawn breath.

Then something bent down and took hold of me and shook me like the end of the world. Whee-ee-ee-ee-ee, it shrilled, through an air crackling with blue light, and with each flash a great jolt drubbed me till I thought my bones would break and the sap fly out of me like a split plant.

I wondered what terrible thing it was that I had done.

From **The Bell Jar**
by Sylvia Plath, 1963

Today

*The poet – a successful black writer – expresses how easy
it is as a successful woman to ignore others who have not
been so lucky.*

A woman with a gash
so deep and wide in
her black soul
came and spilled her
self over me.

Asking to be held
like no-one held her

Asking to be fed
like no-one fed her.

She crawled beneath
my skirt trembling and
afraid and clasped
my lifeboat legs.

But I had meetings
to go to,
and a world to save.

Gabriela Pearse, 1987

Windrush Child

*John Agard is a popular poet and children's writer from
Guyana. He moved to England in 1977. Windrush was
the name of the ship that carried the first immigrants into
Britain to help build the economy.*

85

Behind you
Windrush child
Palm trees wave goodbye

above you
Windrush child
seabirds asking why

around you
Windrush child
blue water rolling by

beside you
Windrush child
your Windrush mum and dad

think of storytime yard
and mango mornings

and new beginnings
doors closing and opening

will things turn out right?
At least the ship will arrive
in midsummer light

and you Windrush child
think of grandmother
telling you don't forget to write

and with one last hug
walk good walk good
and the sea's wheel carries on spinning

and from that place England
you tell her in a letter
of your Windrush adventure

stepping in a big ship
not knowing how long the journey
or that you're stepping into history

bringing your Caribbean eye
to another horizon
grandmother's words your shining beacon

learning how to fly
the kite of your dreams
in an English sky

Windrush child
walking good walking good
in a mind-opening
meeting of snow and sun

John Agard, 1998

A near-death experience

Jan Mark wrote stories about ordinary people caught in extraordinary settings. This extract comes from a novel about imaginary events related to the millennium year, 2000.

As Near Death Experiences go it had been irregular, as he discovered when he read up on the subject afterwards. Everyone else who died and rose again was permitted a glimpse of heaven, was greeted by long-dead loved ones, welcomed effusively and then abruptly shown the door when some doctor galvanized the failing heart. He did not believe in an afterlife. When he saw the articulated truck waltzing side-on across the central reservation he had expected to be extinguished. But he was not dead, only sleeping. If he had had a vision it had not been of heaven or of hell, therefore it must have been a dream.

Up to a point his experiences tallied with the accounts in the books. He had risen above the snarled traffic, the converging police cars, fire-engine and ambulance, to look down upon the fuming tangle of mashed steel in which he supposed his mangled body lay leaching life. Drifting upward and backward. He was so enjoying the sensation that he failed to notice when the sky thickened and closed in and he found himself in a softly luminous tunnel from which he had emerged not into an Elysian garden but in a broad city square with a fountain, formal flower-beds, ornamental trees, surrounded by public buildings. Through the trees he saw a great gate and a tower, limpidly blue, but there was no time to look. On the steps of a church sat a group of people. They noticed him, beckoned to him, and without walking, without any effort at all, he approached the steps, moving through a lilac twilight that was not dusk or daybreak but noon, for almost overhead hung a black sun, and he did not think it strange.

The people on the steps arose and held out their arms. They were long-haired, men and women alike, wearing robes, jewellery, trailing scarves, and they were not his long-dead loved ones. He had never seen any of them before in his life. He reached the foot of the steps and was about to ascend to those welcoming faces, the outstretched arms, when something caught him by the elbow. He half turned, half saw behind him an urgent presence, an impression of long swinging skirts, bright floating hair, mouthing something as it tugged his sleeve. 'No, it is too soon. It is much too soon. You must come away.'

He thought, remembered thinking, I was wrong, this is heaven, they let me see it and now I am being dragged to hell. He gazed back imploringly at the yearning welcoming beings as if they might save him. One, a shining golden woman, came down a step or two and said, 'Go now, we'll meet again.'

He cried despairingly, 'Where?' and she answered, 'Why here, in Kantoom, under the black sun, at the end of a thousand years.'

He was not going to hell, he had not been in heaven; he had been in Kantoom, but his frantic companion was dragging him away, no time for questions, he was alone, he was back in the tunnel, he was lying at the side of the green Mercedes that had picked him up on the slip-road to the M40, and a voice was saying, 'He'll do. The other one's gone.'

From **The Eclipse of the Century**
by Jan Mark, 1999

The Publishers would like to thank the following for permission to reproduce copyright material:

Photo credits

p.4 © 2007 The British Library; **p.7** Trinity College Library, Cambridge; **p.9** © Mary Evans Picture Library/Alamy; **p.14** ©Renaissance Films, Courtesy of the Ronald Grant Archive; **p.19** © 2003 Topham Picturepoint; **p.25** © 2007 The British Library; **p.26** ©

Acknowledgements

pp.66–70 extract from *Pygmalion* (1913). Reprinted by permission of The Society of Authors, on behalf of the Bernard Shaw Estate; **pp.72–73** 'Cargoes' from *Collected Poems* (William Heinemann, 1924). Reprinted by permission of The Society of Authors as the Literary Representative of the Estate of John Masefield; **pp.76–78** extracts from 'The Hollow Men' from *Collected Poems 1909–1962* (Faber & Faber, 1974); **pp.78–80** extract from "The De Wets Come to Kloof Grange" in *This Was the Old Chief's Country: Stories by Doris Lessing* (Michael Joseph, 1951), copyright 1951 Doris Lessing. Reprinted by kind permission of Jonathan Clowes Ltd., London, on behalf of Doris Lessing; **pp.80–83** extract from *Waiting for Godot* (1952; Faber & Faber, 1966); **pp.83–85** extract from *The Bell Jar* (Faber & Faber, 1966); **pp.85–86** 'Today' from *Daughters of Africa*, edited by Margaret Busby (Vintage, 1993); **pp.86–88** 'Windrush Child' from *Half-caste and other poems* (Hodder Children's Books, 2004), © 1998 by John Agard. Reproduced by kind permission of John Agard c/o Caroline Sheldon Literary Agency Limited; **pp.88–90** extract from *Eclipse of the Century* (Scholastic, 2000). Reprinted by permission of David Higham Associates.

Every effort has been made to trace all copyright holders, but if any have been inadvertently overlooked the Publishers will be pleased to make the necessary arrangements at the first opportunity.